£2·25

C000092401

Practice Perfect

An activity notebook for all young musicians

Susan O'Neill
with illustrations by Todd O'Neill

This practice notebook is for beginner players of any instrument, and is designed to encourage the development of good practising habits right from the first stages of musical learning. The book combines the flexibility of a conventional manuscript book with musical games, puzzles and exercises to help make learning fun.

Each page contains space for *practice notes* where teachers can write their own instructions and reminders, while the manuscript at the bottom of every page can be used for explanations, exercises, or composition and theory practice. There are additional manuscript pages at the end of the book.

On the last page you will find a summary of the musical terms and signs which have been introduced throughout the book.

© 1994 by Faber Music Ltd
First published in 1994 by Faber Music Ltd
3 Queen Square London WC1N 3AU
Illustrations © 1994 by Todd O'Neill
Cover design by Todd O'Neill
Printed in England

ISBN 0 571 51485 5

This book belongs to:

Name: _____

Instrument: _____

Music teacher: _____

Lesson 1

Practice notes:

_____

_____

_____

_____

_____

_____

Which path leads Junior to his **Practice Record?**

Make your own **Practice Record**. Each day you practise, put a mark on a calendar using coloured pencils, pens or stickers.

Lesson 2

Practice notes: _____

Music is written on a **staff** or **stave.**

Lines	Spaces

1 2 3 4 5   1 2 3 4

Fill in the blanks: There are ____ lines and ____ spaces.

Draw a note on every line.   Draw a note in every space.

1 2 3 4 5   1 2 3 4

Draw a circle around every **line** note and a square around every **space** note.

Lesson 3

Practice notes:

Is your posture and position **perfect?**

T R E B L E   C L E F

Draw a treble clef on each staff below.

Can you find 10 treble clefs hidden in this drawing of the composer **Beethoven?**

Did you know...?

Ludwig van Beethoven (1770 -1827) was completely deaf during the later part of his life, but he continued to compose and produced many of his greatest works.

Lesson 4

Practice notes: _____

_____

_____

_____

_____

Remember to *count!*

Draw a line from each instrument to its name.

Can you find all the instruments on this page in the word search below?

W	T	M	U	S	R	E	C	O
O	C	R	A	O	I	V	T	N
R	L	T	U	R	A	E	R	E
D	M	C	L	N	N	I	U	T
S	P	U	F	I	R	R	M	N
E	I	V	R	L	A	V	P	I
A	B	A	O	T	U	V	E	L
R	L	O	I	P	D	T	T	O
C	L	U	V	E	E	C	E	I
H	G	A	R	I	R	T	R	V
R	E	C	O	R	D	E	R	E

VIOLIN

CLARINET

GUITAR

TRUMPET

RECORDER

FLUTE

Did you know...? All the instruments on this page play music in the **treble clef**.

Lesson 5

_____

_____

_____

_____

_____

_____

Play *slowly* at first.

Parts of the Grand Piano

lid

keyboard

piano stool or bench

lid prop

pedals

Unjumble the letters to find out more about the piano.

1. The grand piano has 88 _ _ _ _ (eysk).

2. The keys are either black or _ _ _ _ _ (hiwet).

3. A _ _ _ _ _ _ (mamhre) hits the string inside the piano to make the sound.

4. The whole set of keys is called the _ _ _ _ _ _ _ _ (arkybeod).

5. The _ _ _ _ _ _ (eadslp) near the floor are pushed down.

Did you know...? The first piano was invented in the year 1710 by an Italian named *Bartolomeo Cristofori*. He called it **piano e forte** because it could produce notes which were both soft and loud.

Lesson 6

Practice notes: _____

_____
_____
_____
_____
_____

Make sure you are playing the **correct** notes!

B A S S 𝄢 C L E F

Some instruments read music in the bass clef.
The piano plays in both treble and bass clefs!

Draw a bass clef on each staff below.

Can you name each of the notes below?

This note is held for **4 counts**. It is called a

_____.

These notes are held for **2 counts** each. They are called

_____.

These notes are held for **1 count** each. They are called

_____.

Play slowly at first until you are sure all your notes are correct, and then gradually increase the speed. Count the number of times you can play a piece or a difficult section *perfectly*.

If you don't understand a sign or term on your music, look it up in the back of this book or ask your teacher to explain it.

Lesson 7

Practice notes: _____

_____

_____

_____

_____

_____

Remember to *listen* carefully!

Which instrument is being recorded?

If you have a tape recorder, try recording yourself as you play!

Music is divided into **bars** or **measures** by **bar lines**. At the end of a piece or section there is a **double bar line**.

bar line   bar   double bar line

Multiple choice

1. What sort of music do you like best?

a) jazz   b) pop   c) classical

d) rock   e) a mixture

f) other: _____

2. How many instruments do you have at home?

a) 1   b) 2   c) 3   d) more than 3

Name the instrument(s): _____

_____

Lesson 8

Practice notes: _____

_____

_____

_____

_____

_____

Begin your practice with a warm-up!
All performers warm-up before they begin.
An athlete warms-up before every work-out,
and most musicians play warm-up exercises
at the beginning of each practice session.
If you don't have a warm-up exercise, ask
your teacher, or try writing your own.

This is called a **Stem** →

Notes above the middle
line have stems that
point **down**.

Notes below the middle
line have stems that
point **up**.

Stems of notes on the
middle line may point
either **up** or **down**.

Can you name each of these musical signs?

1. Treble clef _____
2. _____
3. _____
4. _____
5. _____
6. _____
7. _____

Lesson 9

Practice notes: _____

Be *patient*, you will soon improve!

Notes and Rests

Rests are signs of musical 'silence'. They tell you not to play for a certain number of counts or beats. Each note has a rest with the same value. Can you fill in the number of counts for each note and rest below?

(o) = (▬) _____ counts each.

(♩ ♩) = (▬ ▬) _____ counts each.

(♪ ♪) = (𝄽 𝄽) _____ count each.

Did you know....?

The **saxophone** was invented in 1840 by Adolphe Sax. Although it is made of brass, it is a woodwind instrument because it uses a single reed like the clarinet.

True or False?

1. The saxophone is a brass instrument.   True / False

2. The violin is a string instrument.   True / False

3. The flute reads music in the bass clef.   True / False

4. The trumpet is a brass instrument.   True / False

5. The grand piano has 88 keys.   True / False

Lesson 10

Practice notes: _____

Play as if you are giving a **performance!**

INSTRUMENT WORDSEARCH

W	P	U	R	C	E	L	L	O	C	E	R	T	T	S
O	T	F	G	U	I	T	A	R	N	T	T	C	R	A
R	E	O	L	V	D	R	A	O	B	Y	E	K	O	N
D	N	B	I	U	T	R	H	U	M	S	P	E	M	O
S	I	O	C	U	S	P	D	O	O	V	M	Y	B	O
E	R	E	D	R	O	C	E	R	I	M	U	B	O	S
A	A	X	C	X	E	T	D	O	U	I	R	F	N	S
R	L	A	A	X	U	R	L	R	T	M	T	L	E	A
C	C	S	V	L	P	I	A	N	O	G	S	V	S	B
H	O	I	F	U	N	O	R	I	A	B	U	T	U	O

BASSOON • CELLO • CLARINET • DRUMS • FLUTE • GUITAR
KEYBOARD • OBOE • PIANO • RECORDER • SAXOPHONE
TROMBONE • TRUMPET • TUBA • VIOLIN

Lesson 11

Practice notes: _____

_____

_____

_____

_____

_____

Listen carefully to everything you play.

Listen carefully to any piece of music and then write or draw what the music makes you think about.

Time signatures

The numbers at the beginning of every piece are called the **time signature**.

The top number tells you how many counts or beats are in every bar. $\frac{4}{4}$

In $\frac{2}{4}$ there are ___ counts in every bar.

In $\frac{3}{4}$ there are ___ counts in every bar.

In $\frac{4}{4}$ there are ___ counts in every bar.

When you play music you need to count and keep a steady speed or tempo. Use a **metronome** to help you count and keep time.

Lesson 12

Practice notes: _____

Are you playing the **correct** notes and rhythms?

QUIZ

Fill in the missing words.

1. A person who writes music is a _____.

2. A music staff has ___ lines and ___ spaces.

3. Bar lines divide the music into _____.

4. At the end of a piece there is a _____ _____ line.

5. Music can be written in the treble or bass _____.

6. At the beginning of a piece there is a _____ _____.

7. The musical sign for silence is called a _____.

8. The musical alphabet has ___ notes.

Answers: clef • 7 • time signature • composer • 4 • bars • 5 • rest • double bar

Lesson 13

Practice notes: _____

_____

_____

_____

_____

_____

Can you play *fast* and *slow*?

The words at the beginning of a piece tell you what speed or *tempo* you should play.

Slow	**Medium**	**Fast**
lento	moderato	allegro

The **fastest** piece I can play is _____.

The **slowest** piece I can play is _____.

Write your own composition

Use the manuscript below to write a piece about something that interests you. Follow these instructions:

1. Put the clef at the beginning of every line.

2. Write the tempo at the beginning of your piece.

3. Choose a time signature and make sure your notes add up to the correct number of counts or beats in every bar.

Did you know....?

The composer **Franz Schubert** (1797-1828) wrote this piece using cats instead of notes.

Lesson 14

Practice notes: _____

_____

_____

_____

_____

_____

_____

Five of the fish below have musical signs which are mistakes.
Can you find them all?

Lesson 15

Practice notes: _____

Be *organized* when you practise!

Which brass instrument leads to the notes?

① ② ③ ④

Write the number in these circles which matches each of the brass instruments on this page.

◯ french horn   ◯ trombone

◯ trumpet   ◯ tuba

Lesson 16

Practice notes: _____

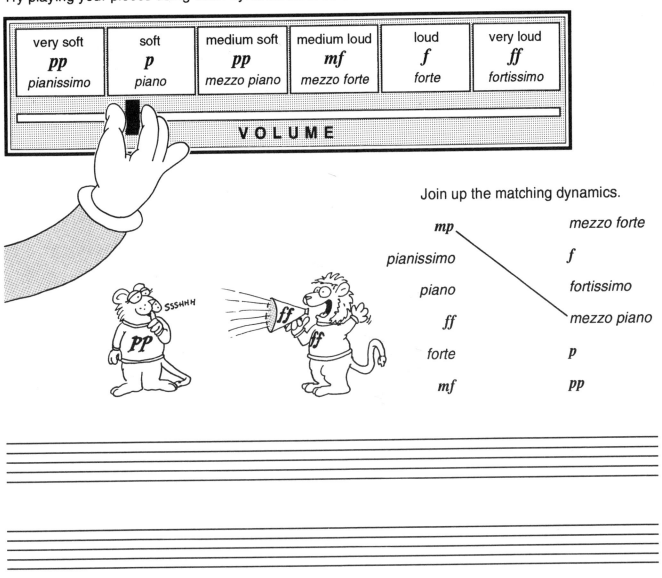

These **dynamic** markings tell you to play loud or soft.
Try playing your pieces using each dynamic level below.

very soft *pp* pianissimo	soft *p* piano	medium soft *pp* mezzo piano	medium loud *mf* mezzo forte	loud *f* forte	very loud *ff* fortissimo

VOLUME

Join up the matching dynamics.

mp — mezzo forte

pianissimo — f

piano — fortissimo

ff — mezzo piano

forte — p

mf — pp

Lesson 17

Practice notes: _____

_____
_____
_____
_____
_____
_____

Notation Crossword

Across

4. This note is held for ___ count.

5. This rest is held for ___ counts.

7. This is a bass _____.

8. This is a _____.

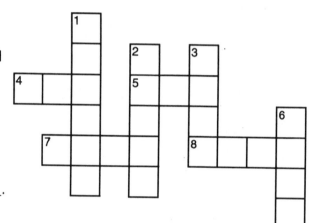

Down

1. This is a _____ clef.

2. This is a _____.

3. This note is held for _____ counts.

6. The line on this note is called a _____.

Write one note with the same value as:

♩ + ♩ = __

♩ + ♩ = __

♩ + ♩ + ♩ = __

♩ + ♩ + ♩ + ♩ = __

If you practise slowly and carefully, you will make faster progress!

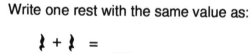

Write one rest with the same value as:

𝄽 + 𝄽 = __

▬ + ▬ = __

𝄽 + 𝄽 + ▬ = __

𝄽 + 𝄽 + 𝄽 + 𝄽 = __

Lesson 18

Practice notes: _____

_____

_____

_____

_____

_____

_____

There are eight musical signs hidden in this drawing of the composer **Vivaldi**. Can you find them all?

bass clef
flat
natural
note
rest
sharp
staff
treble clef

Check your posture and position.

Sharp • Flat • Natural Signs

This is a **sharp** ♯
A sharp raises a note one semitone.

This is a **flat** ♭
A flat lowers a note one semitone.

This is a **natural** ♮
A natural cancels a sharp or flat.

When sharps or flats appear at the beginning of a piece, they are called a **key signature.**

Did you know...?

The baroque composer **Antonio Lucio Vivaldi** (1678 - 1741) wrote nearly 500 concertos including the famous *Four Seasons* for solo violin and orchestra.

Lesson 19

Practice notes: _____

_____

_____

_____

_____

_____

Listen carefully and make the best sound you possibly can!

Listen to the character or style of the piece you are playing. Is it happy or sad, bouncy or calm? Try to play your piece in different ways and listen carefully to how you vary the mood or style each time you play it.

Which cassette tape is being played?

VIVALDI BEATLES BEETHOVEN THE BLUES BROTHERS MOZART ELVIS PRESLEY

Lesson 20

Practice notes: _____

_____

_____

_____

_____

_____

_____

Let's hear your best ***performance!***

Before playing for a concert or exam, make sure you can...

• keep a steady tempo

• play the correct notes and rhythms

• play all the dynamics

• play all the markings in the music correctly

• give a musical performance

• make the best sound possible!

Draw a picture of your instrument below.

 **Did you know ...?**

The Bach family produced seven generations of musicians. The most famous was the composer **Johann Sebastian Bach** (1685-1750) who is playing the keyboard in this picture with members of his family gathered around him.

Some Musical Terms and Signs

Music is written on a **staff** or **stave**.
There are 5 lines and 4 spaces.

Music is divided into **bars** or **measures** by **bar lines**.
At the end of a piece there is a **double bar line**.

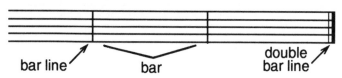

bar line   bar   double bar line

Musical notes are named after the first seven letters of the alphabet.

Note names   Line notes   Space notes

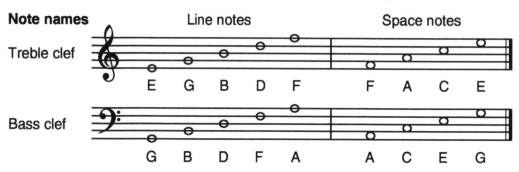

Treble clef

E   G   B   D   F   F   A   C   E

Bass clef

G   B   D   F   A   A   C   E   G

Note lengths

whole note or *semibreve* 𝅝 = 4 counts

half note or *minim* 𝅗𝅥 = 2 counts

quarter note or *crotchet* ♩ = 1 count

Rests are sign of musical 'silence'. Each note has a rest with the same value.

whole note or *semibreve* rest (4 counts)   half note or *minim* rest (2 counts)   quarter note or *crotchet* rest (1 count)

Accidentals

♯   Sharp

♭   Flat

♮   Natural

Key signatures

Time signatures

2/4 - 2 counts in every bar

3/4 - 3 counts in every bar

4/4 - 4 counts in every bar

Tempo or speed

lento (slow)
moderato (medium)
allegro (fast)

Dynamic levels

pp   = *pianissimo* (very soft)

p   = *piano* (soft)

mp   = *mezzopiano* (moderately soft)

mf   = *mezzoforte* (moderately loud)

f   = *forte* (loud)

ff   = *fortissimo* (very loud)